CH00977624

Money Making Ideas for Kids

Starting Your Own Business-A Guide for Teen

Entrepreneurs

Table of Contents

Note for parents

It's never too soon to encourage your kids to be innovative and self-sufficient. And once your child hits the teen years, there are plenty of opportunities to earn money by doing odd jobs, or even by establishing a small home-grown business.

This is a great opportunity for your teen to develop and strengthen his/ her individual skills and interests with a practical goal in mind. Is your teen interested in music or dancing? Is he/she clever with tools and hands-on tasks? Does he/she have an entrepreneurial spirit, or is he/she simply keen to earn money to reach a certain goal?

The best way for your teen to earn money is by pursuing his/her own interests, whether it is swimming, working with children, working outdoors or on the computer. It is easier to maintain enthusiasm and stay innovative when we are doing something that we love.

This book explores the basics of independent jobs for teens, so they can set up a business that is rewarding and enjoyable while paving a path into their chosen future.

The book discusses 18 job ideas as well as a guide to help teens, or kids, get started in their own business. Ideas discussed include:

- legal and safety considerations
- Federal working laws
- writing a business plan
- how to ask for money
- quotes and invoices
- how to decide if a job is for you

First things first

There are a few important aspects of any teen money-making enterprise: it should be realistic, it should be legal and it should be safe.

Keeping it real

Encourage your teen to stick with simple home-grown tasks that are easily achieved with immediate payment. If your teen has wild and exciting plans to become a millionaire within a few months, check the finer details of the plan – is it practical and realistic? Does it involve a huge amount of cash to get started? Will he/she lose confidence if the plan doesn't work out as expected?

This guide gives an outline of entrepreneurial paying jobs for teens, so your child should be able to find something that fits his/ her interests. It is important that your teen understands the value of starting small, so they can build experience in a safe environment, among family and friends, rather than setting the parameters too wide in the beginning.

For extremely ambitious teenagers, a business plan is a great way to keep wild ambitions within the bounds of safety and reality. Writing down: "A year from now, I expect to have 50 regular clients and five friends working for me" is more pragmatic than signing up five friends then making wild promises to fifty new customers.

Legal considerations

Help your teen double check that all the legal necessities are in place. Have you reached the legal age for this activity? Do you need a special license or certificate? Should you give receipts for payment? Do you need to pay tax? Finally, make sure your teen is not undertaking risky activities for the sake of making cash.

Once you've established that the money-making idea is practical and safe, your teen is ready to start business! This book will outline all the different aspects of making money independently, and will also provide some ideas on how your teen can set up a business, keep it running and keep it profitable.

Federal Working Laws in the US

It is important to monitor your teen's working hours to ensure he/ she still has time to attend to school work comfortably and also to be sure you are not violating federal working laws.

Working Laws – Children aged under 14

For children under the age of 14, federal law forbids certain jobs and restricts children from working any regular job that requires mandatory appearance and compulsory hours. However, the following casual jobs are permitted for children aged 14 and under:

Retail

Sales

Acting

Delivery person

Non-hazardous farm work

Office and clerical duties

Working Laws – Children aged 14 to 15

Children aged 14 to 15 years old are restricted in the hours they are permitted to work. While they are legally permitted to work until 9pm during the summer, during the school year they are not allowed to work:

Before 7 am or after 7 pm

More than three hours per day

More than eighteen hours per week

.

Working Laws – Children aged 16 to 17

State laws can vary about the restrictions on specific working hours. For example, some states will not allow children aged 16-17 to work past 9pm, so make sure you are aware of your state laws before your child starts working.

Children aged 16 and 17 are restricted for working in hazardous workplaces, which are defined as working in the vicinity of:

Meat slicers

Saws

Grinders

Patty-making machines

Choppers

Safety considerations

In the early days of your teen's business, you will need to supervise fairly closely. After all, your teen will be going into strangers' homes and requesting cash in return for work, so there are several obvious hazards.

Start by only allowing your teen to work with people known to you, and as the business expands, make sure you meet the potential customers and know exactly where your teen is working, and how long they expect to be there.

Make sure your teen is experienced and comfortable with any machinery he/ she is expected to use in the course of his/her duties. Remind your teen to wear safety glasses when necessary.

Some expenses are outside the teen's responsibility and fall upon you as the parent to ensure your child is safe. If your teen needs to drive a vehicle as part of his job, then as a parent you need to be confident this vehicle is roadworthy at all times. You don't want your teen to postpone fixing faulty brakes just because he hasn't earned enough money yet.

Taxation requirements

Once your child is earning more than $5700 per year, he/she must file an Internal Revenue Service tax return on the earnings. The task of filling out a tax return is valuable business lesson besides being an important milestone in any business enterprise.

Starting Your Own Business

You're ready to start your own business! Congratulations!
This guide will help you look at the business potential of
your interests and aspirations. You will explore how to
build up valuable experience, how to promote your new
business and how to charge your clients.

Writing a Business Plan

Before you launch into work, start by writing up a business
plan.

A business plan helps you articulate what you want to
achieve from your business, whether you want to build
experience in a certain field, or earn a certain amount each
week, or simply have the perfect excuse to stay outdoors
near the water all summer.

By writing down your plan, you can ensure your business
stays on track so it is consistently rewarding. Even adults
can find themselves side-tracked by the challenge of
pursuing new customers or more money, when these goals
can distract you from the reason you actually started the
business in the first place.

The other positive aspect about writing a business plan is
that you recognize the tasks you need to complete before

you start building up your business. For example, you might need to build up experience and research realistic fees before you start working professionally.

What are your long-term goals?

Your first business is an important stepping stone towards the next phase of your life. So what do you hope to achieve from building this business? There are no wrong answers!

What service will you provide?

What exactly do you want to do in order to make money? If you don't know yet, look through this guide for some inspiration.

Do you have the skills to provide this service?

Once you have decided on the service you will provide, check that your skills and experience are appropriate for you to do this professionally. If you simply need to build experience, spend six months volunteering for family and close friends, so you are confident and capable before you start expanding into the professional market. Check the legal requirements carefully, and work towards achieving any certificates you might need before you can work legally at your chosen service.

How much will you charge for your service?

Do some research before you decide on what you will charge. Always stay within realistic market rates – if you make your services too cheap, you will enjoy no financial reward for your work, and if you are too expensive, you won't pick up new work.

Figure out some innovative ways to offer discounts, as people love to get a bargain occasionally!

How many hours a week do you plan to work?

It is very important to work this out before you start accepting work. If your business proves to be popular, it can be difficult to turn down work opportunities. But if you start with a clear plan – for example: "I will work up to 3 hours a day on Saturdays and Sundays and 1 hour a day during the week/ no more than 5 hours in total on weekdays" – then it is easier to turn down work by explaining that all your available work hours are filled. When calculating your available work hours, add up your homework time, your time with friends, and any extra-curricular activities. You also need a few hours each week where you have absolutely nothing to do at all unless you feel like it!

Do you need any tools? Are there any start-up costs?

A good business plan includes outgoing expenses, such as the First Aid course you need to complete or the snow shovel you must purchase before you start work. Don't rush out and buy every item you could possibly need – start small and buy things as you find you need them.

If you calculate these costs, you can approach your parents for a loan to cover them, with the promise that you will pay a certain amount of your earnings until the debt is cleared. This is good business practice, and it is most beneficial to present your parents with a list of essential expenses next to a chart of your intended earnings (hourly rate multiplied by the number of hours you plan to be working each week). Printed promotional materials such as flyers or business cards are a good investment after you have started your job and you're sure you are committed to continuing on this path.

What will you do with your earnings?

First of all, you need to remember that not all your earnings are profit. If you need to drive a car in order to do your job, then the first thing you do with your earnings is fill your car with petrol again.

Calculate your business expenses and subtract this amount

from your earnings. The money left over is your profit.
This is the fun part of working!

At first, your profit might not seem very much money but it
will grow. There will be some weeks where you earn more
money than others. In order to be truly independent, you
should always have some money set aside for when you
earn less money than usual.

A good rule of thumb is to place one third of your profits
into a savings account that you cannot touch. In your
everyday account always have a "float" of one week's pay,
so you are prepared for any unexpected emergency.

Write your weekly earnings in an account book so you can
keep track of how much you are earning and how much
money you are investing back into your business by
purchasing equipment, petrol, advertising material or other
items. These figures will be important if you find you are
earning enough to pay tax.

Write a Plan of Action

Once you have an answer to all the above questions, you
can write up a Plan of Action. This is the list of things you
need to do to launch your business. Set a time-frame and a
deadline for each task. For example, give yourself 2
months to complete your certification. Allocate a certain

length of time to build up the business slowly from one regular client to 10 regular clients, and set certain milestones along the way, such as different advertising campaigns to attract new customers.

If you are borrowing money for start-up costs, allocate a certain amount of time to pay this back. Keep all your goals realistic and modest, so you have a sense of achievement rather than frustration as your business grows.

How to ask for money

You're in business to make money but let's face it – you might feel awkward asking for money. And unfortunately, you will encounter some customers who simply don't want to pay.

This is fine if you are working in a supermarket – if the customer changes his mind about buying the can of soup, he can put it back on the shelf. But once you've mowed his lawn or washed his car or tutored his son, he can't give you your time back.

You need to be confident and professional when you remind people that they have to pay for your services. Like anything, preparation and practice will get you a long way.

Quotes and invoices

Keeping a written record of the money side of your business relationship with a customer is good business practice. A **quote** is a written record you give the customer before you start work – you write down exactly what you intend to do and how much it will cost. The client should agree to your quote before you start work, preferably by signing the quote. If he's not happy with the amount, you can negotiate a few changes on paper.

An **invoice** is the bill. It itemizes the services you have completed, along with the cost now due. If you have already written a quote, the invoice should look exactly the same as the quote approved by the customer.

Play fair

When you charge by the hour, it is important to agree with the client upfront how many hours you intend to work. For example, if you agree that it will take one hour to clear the leaves from the garden, you can't ethically tell the client two hours later that he owes you twice as much as the agreed amount.

If you realize that it will take longer than intended, take a break before the first hour is up and explain the situation to the client. "I'm sorry – I thought I could clear these leaves in an hour, but it looks like a lot longer job. Would you like me to just work at getting the garden basically straight for you, or do you want me to keep going until it is all complete."

Then the client can decide whether to pay you extra or not. If he decides only to pay you for an hour, don't leave the job looking half-done. Make the garden look tidy and presentable, even if all the leaves are not cleared away.

When you are upfront about these issues, you look like a conscientious worker. If you promise one thing and deliver another, you come across as lazy and just out for the money.

Job Choices for Teens

Paper Delivery

What you do

You report to the newspaper office at a set time each morning of your shift. You will be given a certain number of newspapers along with instructions about delivering them along your specific route.

Suits Personality Type

Paper delivery an excellent first job for any personality – it will teach responsibility and an appreciation for the value of money. You will learn that you need to do the job properly, whatever the weather, in order to be paid.

Benefits

Paper delivery is a simple job that can build confidence and independence among young children. You will learn that you have the ability to earn your own money and make your own decisions – a lesson that will sustain you for a lifetime!

Another great benefit is that you are getting plenty of exercise each day. Exercising in the morning before school can boost your concentration and learning ability throughout the day.

You might also be eligible for a free newspaper subscription or discounts on magazines – a great gift for your mum or dad!

How to charge

The newspaper office will have a set policy for paying delivery staff. You can research rival newspaper companies in the area to see which one offers the best rate.

Tools of the trade

There are few start-up costs before delivering papers, although it helps to have a good bicycle so you can deliver your papers faster.

Becoming an expert

Always monitor how long it takes to complete your route, and try to do it a little faster each time. Take pride in being perfectly accurate so people can find their newspapers on their lawn and they receive the right paper!

Promotion

When you are ready to launch into a career, your paper route experience might not seem relevant, but you should always show it on your CV – the fact that you worked a paper route will show future employers that you are willing to work and take responsibility. Employers like to see that you have a good work ethic and that you are independent.

Distributing Business Flyers

What you do

You post advertising flyers into letter boxes or onto windscreens on behalf of local businesses, such as real estate agents, restaurants, social groups and stores.

Suits Personality Type

This is an excellent job for students who want to choose their own hours while they concentrate on their studies. You must be extremely conscientious and trustworthy, and you also enjoy walking.

Benefits

If you secure contracts for several different companies, you can work all the jobs simultaneously simply by putting six flyers in each letter box rather than one at a time. You can choose your own hours and workload, based on the time you have available.

You will get a great deal of exercise walking around the neighborhood to deliver your flyers.

Tools of the trade

You will find it easier to distribute your flyers over a wide area if you drive. However, not all flyers are dropped into letter boxes. If you need to post the flyers on a telegraph poles or notice boards, you will need a staple gun, thumb tacks and tape.

How to charge

Before deciding on your price, research the going rate for flyer delivery in your area. Work out how you will charge, either at a set rate for a certain number of flyers, or according to the distance you travel. Don't forget to calculate in your petrol costs and the time involved.

Becoming an expert

Start with a few smaller businesses so you have an idea how long it takes you to distribute a certain quantity of flyers. As small businesses will not have regular work, you will learn how to pace yourself without too much pressure. Once you are comfortable with your work, you can branch out working for larger companies and you will have a better idea how much work you can take on within your spare time. Explore your neighborhood so you know where all the best places to distribute flyers such as all-day car parks and shopping centers.

Promotion

Demonstrate your skill and dedication by distributing your own flyers promoting your Flyer Distribution Service. Do a letter box drop along the local business strip and don't forget to talk to schools and churches – they will only need flyers distributed occasionally for special events, so they will be glad to have your name on file.

Kids Window Washing Service

What you do

You offer a comprehensive window washing service for neighbors and locals. To clean the windows thoroughly, you must spray the entire surface of the window with water, then scrub the window with a long-handled sponge to remove any dirt or grime before removing excess water with a squeegee. Finally, you spray the entire surface with glass cleaner to make it gleam, then use the squeegee again to remove any further excess and prevent streaking.

Suits Personality Type

This is a great first time job for someone hard-working and conscientious about details. You must be fairly experienced with washing windows, so practice at home first and encourage constructive criticism from your family.

Benefits

This is a fairly straightforward job, and you can set your own hours. It's also an excellent job for a team, so you can set up a group business with a few like-minded friends and share the workload. Your team could consist both younger and older kids, so you have someone to safely climb ladders and tackle high windows.

Tools of the trade

You will need a long-handled sponge or window scrubber, effective window cleaning solution and a rubber squeegee. It is also helpful to have your own step stool and ladder, to make sure you can reach higher windows. However, always ask an older family member to monitor your safety when you start climbing ladders for the first time at a new customer's house.

How to charge

You can charge a certain amount per window, with a smaller fee for smaller easy-to-reach windows. Always give a clear quote to your customer before you begin, based on exactly how many windows are to be cleaned and whether they are small or large. It is a useful business practice to write all this down and add it up, so the customer can see the full amount and agree in advance.

Becoming an expert

When you are practicing at home, experiment with natural and cost-effective window cleaning solutions such as cleaning vinegar or detergent. If you can find an effective cleaner at a fraction of the price of a commercial cleaner, you will make more profit from your earnings!

You could even market your natural window-cleaning solutions by bottling them nicely and giving complimentary bottles to regular customers or selling large bottles.

Promotion

Place flyers in neighborhood letterboxes and on notice-boards at shopping centers, churches and doctors surgeries. Approach local businesses directly to offer your services and leave your contact details and price list with them. Take your team for a walk around the neighborhood with your basic window-cleaning equipment on a sunny weekend afternoon and offer your cleaning services to anyone in their garden.

Yard Service

What you do

You do odd maintenance and gardening job in the yards of your customers. Your jobs will vary according to the season. In winter, you can shovel snow from paths; in spring, you can rake and clear away brush, or you can weed and plant; in summer you mow lawns; and in fall you rake leaves.

Suits Personality Type

You are extremely energetic and you love working outdoors. You are not intimidated by bad weather, and you are reliable. You would have a great deal of experience working in gardens simply from helping out at home, so you know how to complete tasks efficiently and effectively.

Benefits

There is plenty of variety in yard work, as every customer will want something different.

Tools of the trade

You definitely need sturdy shoes, gardening gloves and safety glasses. You should also come prepared with your own pooper scooper, even if the customer does not have their own dog. In winter it is a good idea to have your own snow shovel, so you can arrive at work prepared to start clearing paths.

Your customer will probably have other necessary tools, such as a rake, hoe, lawn mower or hedge trimmers, but it doesn't hurt to gradually collect the ones you use the most.

How to charge

Set an hourly rate for various duties – for example, an hour of poop-scooping and raking leaves is not as arduous as mowing the lawn or shoveling paths, so adjust your fee accordingly. You could set up package deals, incorporating two or three services into an hour and a half for a fixed price.

When you charge by the hour, it is extremely important that your customer can see you have worked hard, even if you don't fully complete the job within an hour. When you work towards making an obvious difference, the customer is more likely to say: "Yes, I'll pay for another half-hour so you can finish it" but if the garden still a mess because you "need more time" you probably won't be invited back.

Becoming an expert

Your parents are your best guides – ask them to help you learn all the varied tasks involved with yard work. Volunteer to help elderly neighbors so you can build up experience and a reputation.

Be observant and pro-active – your customer might book you simply to rake some leaves, but if you point out that a hedge needs trimming, you might land some extra work.

Stay safe – some of the equipment you are using, such as lawn mowers, can be dangerous if you are careless or not concentrating. Do not use equipment that you are unfamiliar with – you can always invite one of your parents or an older sibling to supervise a new job, so you can be sure you are using the equipment safely and responsibly.

Promotion

Do a letter box drop of flyers around your neighborhood so you can build a local customer base. Give regular customers a fridge magnet business card, so they always know where to find your number when they need help in the yard.

Next time your school or church is running a fundraiser, donate a gift voucher for your services as a prize – anyone would love to win two hours of yard work!

Offer customers a discount on their next booking when they recommend you to another customer.

Cleaner

What you do

A cleaner can offer a wide range of services. You could have a regular monthly appointment to wash windows, or a weekly visit to mop floors and scrub the bathroom. Or you might be called in to declutter and freshen up a house before it goes up for sale, or clear out trash and treasures from a cluttered garage or basement.

Suits Personality Type

You are very meticulous and hard-working and you LOVE to clean! You need good communication skills so you can discuss with your clients what is "trash" and what is "treasure". It helps if you are versatile, so you can take on a range of different jobs, and also that you are diplomatic about other peoples' mess!

Benefits

There are plenty of opportunities to establish regular cleaning jobs, and you can choose your hours to fit around other important aspects of your life. If you have an entrepreneurial spirit, you can expand your business with a few friends, so there is always someone available for a one-off job.

Tools of the trade

You need a practical uniform and covered shoes so you are ready for anything. While many of your clients will have cleaning supplies, you might prefer to take along your own supplies. If you are providing cleaning products, you can opt for frugal natural products such as dishwashing liquid to wash windows or vinegar to wipe surfaces.

Plastic gloves are always useful to have on hand for when you need to handle something unhygienic. Keep some basic supplies, such as garbage bags, absorbent paper towels and a dusting cloth. You might also find it practical to have your own heavy-duty broom and other equipment.

How to charge

Set an hourly rate for basic house-cleaning. You may have a different hourly rate for specific tasks, such as cleaning out a basement/ garage, or simply doing floors and windows rather than scrubbing a bathroom.

Once you have a good idea how long various tasks take, advertise "package deals" such as a 2 hour intensive service, or a 45 minute quick clean. Be very specific about what you guarantee from each package deal, and don't offer a "quick clean" unless you have already seen the house and know it is physically possible!

Becoming an expert

Your central goal as a cleaner is to have the client return and say: "Wow, it looks so much better!" While you might be meticulous about getting the stubborn stain off the cupboard door, you also want the overall results to be strikingly obvious, so don't stress too much about the small details. Develop tricks of the trade to declutter and wipe down, so the room gleams instantly. You can always tell the client, "I really want to work on this stubborn mark back here some more…" and you have another booking! Remember the two basic rules of cleaning: tidy before you clean, and work from top to bottom. This system is far more efficient and ensures you can move on from each spot leaving it clean and tidy without having to go back and remove the cobwebs that fell from the ceiling.

You could expand your business by offering to spruce up houses on the market. Build up contacts in the real estate industry so they can refer clients to you. Go beyond simply cleaning and de-cluttering by collecting a range of cushions, rugs, vases and pictures to give a shabby house a quick "lift" with flowers and extra color.

Promotion

As a cleaner, you don't encourage clutter – so hand out fridge magnets with your contact details rather than business cards. This way, your details are always on display for visitors so they can view your handiwork at the same time. You can build a good reputation by offering discount packages for elderly customers or people suffering hardship. Tell your customers you provide gift certificates, which are useful gifts for new parents or anyone suffering a long term illness. You could also donate a gift certificate to local fundraisers.

Pet Sitting and Dog Walking

What you do

You look after pets when their owners are absent. This can involve anything from feeding and playing with pets while their owners are away, or walking a dog while the owner is at work.

Suits Personality Type

You love animals and you are reliable and attentive, with a strong sense of responsibility.

Benefits

If you love animals, you will be in heaven caring for all the pets in the neighborhood. This is your chance to play with them, pet them and observe them to your heart's content. And rather than paying for their food, you are paid to look after them!

Tools of the trade

If you are dog-walking, you need your own pooper-scooper kit, such as a little shovel and a supply of plastic bags on hand. You can purchase small bag-holders that clip for your waist-band so you always have a good supply.

You should also have a large key-ring, as clients will often give you their keys when they need you to visit their home while they are on holidays. Label each key clearly, with the owner's name although NOT the address. Keep your clients' addresses and contact details listed separately, along with contact numbers for their regular vet in case of emergency.

If you want to include pet grooming in your services, you should buy your own pet grooming tools such as a suitable bath, soaps and brushes.

How to charge

Research the current rates for pet-sitting and dog-walking in your area and work out your fee for specific services. If you are dog-walking, you can base your fee on the amount of time you spend walking the dog.

Becoming an expert

Volunteer to be an overnight sitter for the local pet store. The pet store cannot leave animals alone during the night, so they are always looking for volunteers. This will give you experience with all types of animals, such as snakes, guinea pigs and mice, as well as cute kittens and puppies.

You could also ask if you could volunteer as an assistant at the local vet, so you can at least observe techniques for caring for small or injured animals.

Promotion

Print out flyers promoting your services and distribute them throughout the neighborhood, including the local pet stores, veterinary clinics and churches.

However, the best way to promote your skills is by being seen in action. While you are dog-walking wear a "uniform" of a T-shirt with your own logo and contact details on it. This way, people will recognize instantly that you are a professional, so they are more likely to request your services.

Handyman

What you do

You do odd jobs for people who aren't good with tools – anything from hanging pictures or curtains to repairing fences or installing shelves. Stick with simple carpentry jobs that don't require a license – you might feel capable of installing light fittings or unblocking the kitchen sink, but without the right piece of paper you might find yourself in trouble if things go wrong.

Suits Personality Type

You are capable with a problem-solving mind and you are extremely experienced with tools. You understand the importance of measuring and marking up before you start sawing or nailing. You have pleasant easy-going nature and you don't leave any mess behind you!

Benefits

It's great to have a job where your customers really appreciate you. Your customers will always be extremely grateful, partly because you've solved a major problem for them, making their home life easier, and partly because professional tradesmen are usually extremely unreliable!

You can choose your own hours, so you work around the other important aspects of your life.

Tools of the trade

You need a basic toolkit – hammer, nails, screwdrivers, sandpaper etc. Make sure your actual toolkit is neatly packed and portable. You also need a sturdy uniform and covered boots, so you are dressed practically and professionally.

How to charge

Set a basic hourly rate, but also charge for your time traveling to and from a remote location. If you need to buy materials for the job, ask the client to give you this money up-front, so you are not spending your own money. Quote carefully, so you don't give your client any unpleasant surprises when the bill comes.

Some clients might try to take advantage of you by making every job an emergency that has to be done "right now". In this case, add an "Urgent" fee onto the quote, so they are paying you for the inconvenience of dropping everything to help them. This policy will help clients decide the difference between a real emergency, and a task that can wait until a pre-arranged time.

Becoming an expert

Practice every chance you get, trying new tasks and perfecting your skills. Ask a local handyman if you can spend a day (or a week) as an unpaid apprentice, simply to get a feel for the type of jobs you might be asked to complete.

Investigate training courses, so you can become certified.

Promotion

As well as business cards, put flyers up on notice boards at local churches, retirement homes and shopping malls. You could also drop flyers in letter boxes in your local area. Offer people discounts for referring you to someone else – this will get your business growing!

Volunteer to help people in need, such as elderly people or locals going through a difficult time. This will build up valuable experience, as well as giving you a great reputation.

If you maintain a small client base, you can concentrate on being reliable – this is the best way to compete with professional tradesmen who don't necessarily show up when they promise! You will win plenty of referrals and repeat jobs simply by showing up on time and finishing the job properly.

Kids Car Washing Service

What you do

You wash and detail cars for neighbors and locals.

Suits Personality Type

This is a great first-time job, particularly for someone who loves cars and has a good eye for detail.

Benefits

You can choose your own hours, by making appointments with clients when it suits you. You can also decide where you work, so if it is easier for you to work from home, your clients can come to you!

If you decide to expand your business, you can call in some friends so you are all paid for the cars you wash.

Tools of the trade

You cannot assume that your customers have all the necessary cleaning materials. The basics you will need for the exterior are: car washing liquid; window cleaner; sponges; tire brushes; long-handled scrubber; chrome cleaner; tire blacking; and car wax. For the interior, you need a dustpan and broom as well as a hand-held vacuum to clean the upholstery and carpets.

How to charge

Investigate other local car washing services to find out what they charge and establish a competitive but fair rate for your own services.

You can charge a set fee for each cleaning task – washing the body of the car; windows; internal clean; and a luxury service including wax and tire blacking.

Becoming an expert

Car washing might seem like an elementary task, but it does require skill and experience. You not only want to clean cars thoroughly, you want to be fast – when you're paid by the car, you earn more money when you are fast and efficient.

Start by washing and detailing your parents' cars and then move on to neighbors and other family members. Clean their cars for free in return for constructive criticism about how you can improve your technique. Once you are confident enough, you can start promoting your services for a fee.

Encourage your customers to book a specific time to have their car cleaned. Keep track of your workload with an appointment book – block out the times you do not want to work, and write down every appointment you make.

Allocate more time than you need for each appointment, to give yourself some extra time if necessary.

You can arrange for customers to bring their cars to your home at an agreed time, or you can ask for approval to use an empty car park for a block of time so regular and new customers can drop their cars off without appointments. If you are going to do this, you will want to enlist a few experienced car-washing friends to help you.

Promotion
Print out some flyers and distribute them in neighborhood letterboxes. If you are working at a specific car park on weekends place some posters around so people know to come back for the car washing service. You could also print out some discount cards or discount vouchers: every fifth wash and polish is free, or comes with a bonus wax.

Kids Errand Service

What you do

You help neighbors who are sick or housebound by running simple errands on their behalf. For example, you might purchase a few groceries for the woman across the road who has just had a new baby, or you could pick up a heavy parcel from the post office for the elderly man next door. Some elderly people in your neighborhood might be too frail to go for a walk on their own, so you can help out by walking with them for a short time each afternoon – this gives them some fresh air and valuable exercise, while you are there to make sure they stay safe.

Suits Personality Type

You are compassionate, patient and responsible enough to see plenty of opportunities to help people. You are also a cheerful and relaxed person, so you will brighten up someone's day, simply by dropping in for a short time.

Benefits

An errand service is a great first job as it will help you understand how difficult life can be for others and you will develop healthy instincts for helping others. You will make great friends in unexpected places and this is one job where you will receive sincere thanks for your services.

You have the freedom to choose your own hours, and you can expand the business by calling in a few friends to help you with extra jobs.

Tools of the trade

You need an appointment book to keep track of all your errands, otherwise you might find you are double-booking. You also need to keep track of money you are given for errands, to ensure you give the correct change each time. You will probably need a sturdy shopping bag to carry items from the shops.

How to charge

Many of your customers will be on a very small income, so you cannot expect high pay for your errands. You can set a fee based on the time you spend on each errand, and if you plan your time carefully, you might be able to double-up some errands – take the neighbor for a walk while picking up some groceries for another neighbor.

Becoming an expert

Keep a few notes about each of your customers so you can remember their background and requirements. This way you will remember who needs regular medication and who has trouble walking far. You should also keep a few personal notes about each customer in case there is sensitive information to avoid. For example, don't ask about family if there are no relatives left to visit.

Promotion

Print out flyers to distribute around local aged care homes, churches, pharmacies and day care centers. Visit local doctors to tell them about your service, as they will probably have a few patients who would benefit from an errand service or just a friendly visitor occasionally.

Professional Babysitter

What you do

You take care of small children in their home while their parents are out. Depending on the parents' wishes, you can be responsible for giving the children dinner, helping with homework supervising their baths, putting them to bed or simply playing with them. It goes without saying that you are responsible for keeping the children safe and making sure they don't indulge in any activities that would be forbidden by their parents.

Suits Personality Type

You are extremely responsible and comfortable playing with children while supervising them. You are not easily manipulated but you have plenty of fun activities up your sleeve to make the babysitting experience fun for everyone.

Benefits

You can choose your own hours, and if you build up a few clients you will find yourself with regular work. Best of all, this job doesn't necessarily interfere with your homework or relaxation activities – once the kids are in bed you can watch your favorite movie or read your favorite book… while you are being paid!

Babysitting is great experience if you are planning a career in childcare.

Tools of the trade

For your own peace of mind, you should have a First Aid certificate before looking after other people's children. This will give you the background knowledge to handle any kind of emergency promptly.

You always keep track of the parents' instructions so you know the bed-time routine and you know how to discipline the children appropriately if necessary. Most importantly, you know about any medical issues such as allergies, so you can administer medication when required.

Always have emergency contact phone numbers at hand.

How to charge

You can set a standard hourly rate, perhaps with time-and-a-half after midnight or a certain number of hours. Encourage "easy" clients with discounts at your discretion, if you find you enjoy plenty of study time while the children are asleep.

Becoming an expert

The more experience you clock up, the better you will deal with children of all ages. Don't be squeamish about changing diapers or giving baths, as these tasks will become easier with time. Talk to parents and experienced babysitter to learn tricks for settling babies and games that will keep young children entertained without getting them overexcited before bed time.

Go into partnership with another experienced babysitter so you can fill in for each other if one of you is busy. This way you don't lose your main customers just because you are unavailable once or twice.

Promotion

Post flyers up at pre-schools and day care centers. If you have any qualifications, such as a First Aid certificate or references, then mention these on the flyers.

Make up some magnetic business cards to give your clients, so they can keep your phone number handy on the refrigerator. This way you will be the first person they call when they need a babysitter. Leave some flyers with them in case they want to recommend your services to another family.

Earn Money As A Restaurant Delivery Service

What you do

You deliver take-out meals from the restaurant to the customer's front door. Usually pizza parlors and Chinese restaurants offer restaurant delivery service, although you can contact any local restaurant or grocery store, offering your services.

Suits Personality Type

You should be courteous, efficient and responsible. This is a job for someone who is comfortable on their own. A restaurant delivery service is a deceptively simple job, but you need to have a clear head for direction and priorities, so you can keep all the orders straight and make your deliveries in the shortest possible time.

Benefits

If you are the sort of person who likes collecting anecdotes about your crazy experiences, then this is the job for you! You never know what you will encounter when you knock on the door to deliver a pizza.

Tools of the trade

You need your own car, plus a good knowledge of your local area. You need an excellent driving history, and experience driving in all kinds of weather, day and night. Purchase the latest up-to-date street map, and it wouldn't hurt to invest in a GPS, so you always know the quickest route to take. If you are working for a franchise restaurant or caterer, they may supply a uniform.

A sturdy money belt is useful, and you must have your own phone. Make it a rule to start each shift with a full tank of petrol, as you don't want to worry about running low on gas.

How to charge

Start by calling a few local restaurants employing delivery drivers and ask how much they pay, and how the pay is based. Whether you charge by distance, number of deliveries, or an hourly rate, you need to calculate in your petrol usage. Keep a record of how many miles/ kilometers you travel each shift. This is important even if you do not need to report to your employer about the distance traveled. If you do not calculate this into your fee, you might find you're not earning enough to cover your outgoings. If your hourly rate does not cover your petrol, you need to discuss this with your employer – or find another delivery job with more realistic payment.

Some of your customers will tip you. You will probably be allowed to keep all tips, but check your employer's policy on tipping first.

Becoming an expert

One important rule for food delivery people: Never walk *through* the front door into a person's home. Hand over the meal at the front door and then leave, whether it's a mate's party and he just wants you to say "hi" to everyone, or it's a pleasant lady who asks you to come in for a moment while she finds her purse. Make it a rule to always stay just outside the front door. This is a basic safety rule, besides saving you from the temptation of joining in the party "just for a minute" when you are supposed to be working.

Always have plenty of change so you don't have any awkward encounters. At the same time, always hand over extra cash when report back to base, as you don't want to be responsible for wads of money.

If you have several deliveries, it is wise to invest a few minutes in planning the most sensible route encompassing each address, rather than driving backwards and forwards. This will make your job less stressful, and if you are paid per delivery, it is in your best interest to become as efficient as possible!

Keep your car clean and presentable as this is essentially your "office". A clean car not only presents well, it is also easier to pack deliveries and ensure everything is delivered safely and hygienically.

Promotion

Prepare a business proposal for local restaurants, outlining the hours you are available and quoting a realistic fee. (Research the fee first by researching how much each restaurant pays, and then calculating whether it is a viable fee when offset against petrol costs). Include relevant information, such as your work history, driving history, the fact that you have a driver's license, the type of vehicles you are eligible to drive (they might want you driving a small truck!) and that you have an excellent driving record. Present your business proposal in person to business managers in the area. Make sure you are well-groomed and courteous, and don't expect an answer straight away. As restaurants generally only want part time employees, you could juggle one or two assignments.

Tutoring and Mentoring

What you do

You assist younger or less advanced students with their studies as part of a tutoring program, or on a one-to-one basis.

Suits Personality Type

You are particularly good at a certain subject – such as mathematics, English, science or music – and you have a knack for explaining the key points of a topic to make them clear. You are very patient and you understand that it takes a while to grasp certain concepts so you show respect for students while they try to work it out.

Benefits

You can choose your own hours and perhaps even have students come into your home. Tutoring is also a great way to revise your own lessons as you go back to basics. It is also extremely rewarding when your students suddenly "click" and understand the subject when a professional teacher couldn't explain it to them.

Tools of the trade

You need high grades to prove that you will be a successful tutor. As you will be working with impressionable children younger than you, their parents will expect you to provide a clear background check, along with a social security card, and personal letters of recommendation from non-family members as references.

The most important qualification is experience, so you can start by volunteering at your school in order to establish your routine and approach. If you prove to be a successful tutor, you can gain a valuable reference from your school.

How to charge

You will charge an hourly rate, and as each assignment will be a weekly or bi-weekly job, you can rely on a regular income. Your hourly rate will depend on your experience, so it will gradually increase as you become older.

Ask around to see what people of similar age and experience are charging and keep your rate fair but competitive.

Becoming an expert

Once you have successfully passed your graduation and entrance exams, you will be able to specialize as a tutor and charge a little more. The more special skills you have, such as the ability to speak other languages, will make your job more interesting, varied and provide steady work.

Your goal is to build your student's confidence so they overcome the issues they have with the topic. When you can build a rapport with each student, meeting them half-way to overcome the learning difficulty, then you are truly an expert tutor.

Pair up with other tutors who might have different fields of expertise. This way you can advertise together, or stand in for each other if one is busy or unable to attend the tutoring session.

Promotion

Place flyers on notice boards at high schools and/ or colleges, or in the local newspaper. Apply to help at in-school programs and mentorships, such as programs matching high school students with elementary or junior high students. Check local school websites to see if they are advertising for tutors.

Your best form of promotion is through word-of-mouth. Offer one hour's free tutoring to any students who recommend you to another customer.

Blogging

What you do

You write content for your own web page based on your specific knowledge and passions – this could be anything from book reviews to competitive kite flying. Once or twice a week, you write blogs describing your experiences and you publish articles relating to the topic of your choice. You will achieve a great deal more interest to your site if you include photos and short videos.

Once you establish your web page and update it regularly, you will start receiving offers for advertising. Only accept advertisements for products that complement your web content. You earn a commission whenever viewers to your page purchase a product after clicking on an ad from your site.

Suits Personality Type

You are extremely creative with a passion for writing and a knack for marketing. You also love exploring the Internet.

Benefits

If you are ambitious to establish a writing career, a web page is a great way to showcase your talents and keep working at your craft. The interactive nature of the Internet gives you important feedback about what material attracts viewers and what material they are not interested in.

Once your website is established with plenty of ads, you will have an ongoing income, simply through the effort of maintaining your blog.

Tools of the trade

You need a clear topic, Internet connection and preferably your own computer. An iPhone is also an excellent writer's tool, as you can take pictures as events occur and upload them instantly onto your web page.

You do not need to spend a fortune setting up and designing your own web page – simply set it up through a free site such as WordPress, so you are free to change and modify your content and layout as you wish.

Becoming an expert

There are a few tricks to building traffic to your site, and most of them are based on linking to other similar/ more popular websites on the same topic. So if an expert on your topic is appearing locally, write a blog about meeting this expert, throw in some original photos and create a hyperlink to the expert's page. Or you can quote experts, promote events or comment on articles in the news, based on your experience and perspective.

These strategies add authenticity to your expertise on the topic, so people are more likely to respect your views. They also boost your ranking in search engines so more Internet browsers will stumble across your blog, making you more valuable to advertisers.

Promotion

Start a Facebook page, or other social media, specifically for your blog – add links to relevant articles on the Internet and in the media, and update Facebook every time you write a new blog. You can keep people interested in your Facebook page by regularly posting humorous or thought-provoking material from other pages. Your goal here is to keep people reading your blog! If they stay with your Facebook page, you know they will read your blog regularly.

Read articles and blogs by other experts in your chosen field, and leave comments along with a link to your website. Other readers, who are already interested in the topic, will switch to your website to learn what you have to say. You can establish mutually beneficial relationships with other bloggers and experts, by making links to each other's content. This helps you both build a regular audience.

Online Handicraft Store

What you do

You make your own gift cards, tie-dyed T-shirts or knitted baby clothes and then sell them online through your own website.

Suits Personality Type

You love craft and you make more than you can use. You also have a flair for design so your creations are distinctive and you take pride in making every detail perfect.

Benefits

You have a job you are passionate about and you have complete control over how much you have in-store. If you lose interest in a certain line of handicrafts, you can drop it from the range. If you are keen to increase your earnings, you can expand your range and promotion.

This is an extremely rewarding and beneficial outlet for anyone suffering ill health or low self esteem – you can achieve something practical and build confidence, while working at your own pace.

Tools of the trade

You need all your handicraft materials and plenty of time. In order to sell goods such as baby clothes, you need a range of sizes and colors so you are ready for any order. All your goods should feature your unique label, whether it is a sticker or a clothing tag, which you can have made up by a logo store.

Set up a website with photos of your products along with prices. You could also try promoting a few items on auction sites such as Ebay. If you are posting items to customers, buy all your postage needs in bulk so you aren't constantly running to the post office for more packaging and stamps.

How to charge

When you work out a price for each craft item, start by calculating the cost of materials then assess how much time it would have taken. Don't price yourself out of the market by giving yourself too high an hourly rate.

It's a good idea to have a range of prices to capture both sides of the market – the people with a limited budget and the people who value luxury goods.

Always add postage costs separately, so people pay the exact postage costs to their area on top of the price of the item.

Becoming an expert

Make sure all your goods are the highest quality Start with a small "friends and family" market so you can handle any quality issues directly without any bad feelings. Research the best way to care for your goods over the long term so you can give detailed instructions to customers.

Attend workshops to perfect your craft, and. Always work towards expanding your range as the more items you have for sale, the more likely you are to capture a customer's interest. For example, if you love making bead bracelets, you should also make earrings, pendants and necklaces so you can sell matching sets to one customer, or have a range of items to attract another customer. If you enjoy doing origami, you can make gift cards, lucky charms and children's toys, as well as packaging some unique craft kits for kids who want to learn how to do simple origami.

Set up a stall at local markets so you can build up some regular customers and figure out which craft items most appeal to your target market.

Promotion

Set up a website with plenty of photographs of all your beautiful handiwork. Customers can order items from your website, so you have the option of making whatever is required. Link your website to a Facebook page so you can turn one-time customers into regular customers with regular updates on your latest crafts.

Donate beautiful items to local fundraising auctions to raise your local profile.

Invest some of your budget into unique and striking gift bags to package your goods.

Lifeguard jobs for Kids

What you do

During the months of summer vacation, you work at a swimming pool, a lake, an amusement park or at the ocean, watching over swimmers and responding to emergencies. You must be at least 15 years of age to be a life-guard, and at least 16 years old to work on public beaches.

You should know how to clean a swimming pool and how to test the water, and you can also be responsible for cleaning and tidying change rooms and bathrooms.

Suit personality type

You are a strong swimmer, in peak physical condition and you have a passion for the water. You are calm and observant and you know that swimmers in trouble are not necessarily thrashing around making a lot of noise. You are mature and disciplined enough not to be distracted by your friends while you are on duty. You can also work well as a team, and you don't mind doing some of the more mundane lifeguard duties.

Benefits

Your job involves staying by the pool or the beach all through the glorious summer! This is also a great way to demonstrate responsibility and maturity to future employers.

Tools of trade

You must complete a training course of at least 30- 37 hours duration in order to earn a Lifeguard Certification from The American Red Cross. This certification qualifies you to work at one of the following lifeguard categories:

Traditional lifeguard at a public swimming pool

Waterfront lifeguard at a lake or river resort, or at a swimming pool

Water-park lifeguard at a water-park facility with multiple water activities, or at a traditional swimming pool

Shallow-water Attendant where the water level is up to 4 feet deep

Training courses by the American Lifeguard Association includes professional CPR, rescue and first aid knowledge. Your lifeguard certification has to be renewed every three years, while the CPR, rescue and first aid certificate only lasts for 2 years.

To work at a swimming pool you also need a Pool Operator's Card which certifies that you have all the skills required to maintain pool sanitation and health conditions.

How to charge

There are set salaries for lifeguards, so you won't need to negotiate your own price. As you gain more experience, your salary will increase when you are given greater responsibility.

Becoming an expert

You can never be complacent about your experience or knowledge. Always be on the look-out for advanced training and courses so you can learn more about life-saving.

Promotion

Once you have your qualifications, ask around at local swimming pools, beaches, hotels and resorts. You may need to put your name down at a few places and wait before you are offered a job. Once you have some experience behind you, it will be easier to maintain work. Hotels and resorts with swimming pools often need lifeguards all year around, and they are a great place to build up experience.

A Professional Fundraiser

What you do

You raise money for worthy causes, such as providing extra funds for the local school or library, or raising money for research into a rare disease. Perhaps you'll organize a fun run, a reading relay or a baking competition. Either way, it will be so much fun for such a worthy cause that everyone in your community will love participating and contributing to your efforts.

Suits Personality Type

You are innovative and imaginative, so you can come up with novel exciting ways to catch people's attention so they want to become involved in your fundraising drive. People are always being asked to "give generously" so you need to consistently come up with something different so they want to be involved.

You are also extremely conscientious and trustworthy, as you will be handling other people's money on behalf of a charity. You need to be a great communicator, before, during and after the event so people know where their money is going. You understand the importance of making promises – if you said every participant gets a certificate then you supply certificates.

You have great networking skills so you can talk local businesses into donating prizes for auctions and raffles, and you always acknowledge everyone who helps – this way, they'll help next time too!

Benefits

You have the constant reward that you are helping make the world a better place, both by contributing much-needed funds to worthy causes and by creating a heart-warming and fun community event.

Tools of the trade

Once you have some amateur experience at fundraising, you will need to set up a business in order to take it on professionally. You will need a license and/or authorization to legally collect money on behalf of a charity. If you are collecting on behalf of an established organization, you will need a valid receipt book so your donors can claim their donations for tax purposes.

You also need an enthusiastic team of volunteers who are happy to promote upcoming events on Facebook or in their local community, as well as set up locations, collect donations and help you with every other detail.

Set up a Facebook page with plenty of photos from events you have organized, and include figures to show how many people were involved and how much money was raised. This will show people how versatile you are.

It doesn't hurt to have a few celebrity contacts to pull in extra crowds.

How to charge

The money you raise has to be split into three piles: one covers the charitable contribution, one covers all the expenses, such as materials and advertising, and finally the smallest pile is your fee. You need to be very careful quoting up-front to ensure all expenses are covered so there is enough for an appropriate charitable contribution as well as your fee.

Set up a strict budget for expenses – these should only be a percentage of the money to be donated. Quote a fixed fee for your payment, and make a deal with your client that if the funds raised exceed a certain point, you receive a bonus.

Becoming an expert

Start as a non-professional, helping your local school or church, so you have a feel for how much time is involved in the mundane, behind-the-scenes tasks, and you can see how much money can realistically be raised for various causes.

Advertising can be a huge expense, so you want to be able to promote the event with as little cost as possible – such as through word of mouth and via the Internet.

Promotion

Set up a Facebook page with plenty of photos from events you have organized, and include figures to show how many people were involved and how much money was raised. This will show people how versatile you are.

Performance Artist/ Entertainer

What you do

You love singing, dancing or performing in general and you have perfected a special talent so that now you are good enough to perform in public. Perhaps you are a magician or you are clever at juggling, or perhaps you love being with kids and you're comfortable dressing up as a fairy or a clown!

You could earn some money entertaining children at parties, or performing music at other functions.

Suits Personality Type

You need to be both extroverted and dedicated so you can give an enthusiastic and professional performance every time. You must be professional and reliable as you don't want to let your customers down on an important day.

If you want to entertain children as a clown, magician or fairy, you need to prepare a complete act, lasting at least an hour, so you can keep the children laughing and engaged with your performance.

Benefits

If you have long-term ambitions as an actor or musician, then these regular professional performances will be great practice, as well as bringing in some regular income. You will be working in a great atmosphere, and have the pleasure of being an important part of other peoples' celebrations.

Tools of the trade

If you are planning to work as a musician, you always need to be sure your instrument is ready to go, fully tuned, with spare strings or reeds. As a musician or singer, you need to be able to play requests, so practice regularly and make sure you have a good repertoire of classic songs and current favorites.

As a magician, clown or fairy for children's parties, you need plenty of props to keep the children entertained. Practice your entire act with your own family or in front of a mirror, so you can perfect your performance.

How to charge

Set an hourly rate, so you can tell your customers exactly how much they need to pay. If you're not sure of your hourly rate, call a few local entertainers and ask them for a quote. This will give you an idea what your competition is charging, although in the beginning you should aim for a competitive fee so you can build up experience.

Becoming an expert

As a children's entertainer, you can expand your performance by becoming an expert in making balloon animals or face-painting. This will give you an extra half-hour at each party, increasing your final fee.

As a musician or singer, you can add some creativity to your performance by pretending to be a member of the audience or even a waiter until you suddenly start to play.

Promotion

Always have business cards and flyers available to hand out to guests so you can book more parties. Set up a website, and ask customers for permission to include photographs from their event. While some people might not be comfortable with their photos on the web, others will be thrilled to be up there! And this will give potential customers a glimpse of your great act!

You could even make a short YouTube video of your performance.

Look for opportunities to volunteer your talents at fundraising events, retirement homes or children's hospitals. This type of exposure is invaluable as a means to give you a high profile and it gives you a great opportunity to practice your act.

Party Planner/ Host

What you do

When your neighbor's 5 year old twins want a combined Ben 10/ Dora the Explorer party, you jump into action, offering suggestions for decorations, party bags, themed games and birthday cakes. You prepare all the decorations and games in advance then you supervise the children throughout the party, ensuring everyone has a great time. Once you have one successful party under your belt, you might be asked to do another – perhaps a 21st with a "bubble" theme or a kid's disco party.

When you agree to plan/ host a party, start by giving your clients a standard questionnaire. Who is the party for? What is the date/ time of the party? Where exactly will it be held? How many guests are attending? What is the theme of the party? What are you responsible for as planner/ host (decorations/ games/ gift bags/ supplying the cake)? In the lead-up to the party, make sure you contact your client a few times to update them on what you've been doing. This will help keep everything organized and smooth out any last minute problems or misunderstandings. If you need to decorate before the party, make it very clear when you need to be at the venue.

Suits personality type
You need to be very energetic with contagious enthusiasm and great organizational ability in order to keep everyone entertained for several hours. You should also be able to handle an emergency crisis with style, so you can breeze through problems like a missing birthday cake or badly behaved children.

You need to be very conscientious about delivering what you promise. It's easy to come up with fantastic ideas for a party – it's another thing to actually do the work and follow through on what you have promised.

You should also be confident and comfortable working with children, and know how to work with a schedule, so you know when to blow up the balloons, how long to play each game, and when to settle everyone down in time for the birthday cake.

You can harness a highly creative streak into making inventive gift bags for guests or setting up unique decorative party rooms.

Benefits

If you love basking in a party atmosphere, then you will be in heaven, planning parties for a living. If you have an entrepreneurial spirit, then there are plenty of opportunities to expand your business, take on assistants and partners.

Tools of the trade

You need to know all the bulk-buy warehouses for balloons, decorations and party favors. When you buy in bulk, you can be eligible for a discount or wholesale price, but be careful in the beginning that you don't overstock on things you might never use again. Bulk-buying also saves you running around doing the same errands before each party.

You can take the initiative and prepare party bags in advance, offering these generic bags at a discount price, or using them for a last-minute emergency.

If you have a colored printer, you can design your own unique invitations on behalf of your customers. Don't forget to include your business details in small print on the invitation, so guests know who organized their great party!

Pre-made party packs, decorations, access to bulk warehouses. Color printer to make bright original invitations.

How to charge

Give your clients a quote for your services before the party. To calculate the quote, set yourself a fixed hourly rate and calculate a fixed rate for a party that covers the time you spend preparing for the party beforehand. You will need to charge for expenses, such as decorations, separately, and it is best if you can show receipts for all these items. Do not mark up the price you've spent on decorations – you are covered for your shopping time in your fixed rate.

Becoming an expert
Start by planning parties for friends or family members. Look into all the details from invitations, themes, catering ideas and work out what you can take on and what are not covered by your services. For example, if your services do not include catering, or you can team up with someone who can provide food.

Promotion

At every party, hand out business cards or A5 business flyers with your details. Set up a website and Facebook page and ask your first clients for permission to post photos promoting the work you've done. Offer specials for "the first party booked in June" or "refer a friend".

More Ideas for making Money

- sell cupcakes -you'll need a license
- write ebooks and sell online through kindle or a website
- design graphics, brochures or presentations
- sew pillows or pillowcases
- sell photography on stock photography sites
- make your photos into greeting cards to sell
- start an ironing business- many people don't like or have the time to iron shirts or pants
- Laundry services- do others laundry and deliver fresh, clean, folded clothes back to them
- paint houses, bedrooms, or furniture
- have a special skill? try provide help to others through fiverr.com or elance.com
- teach English through Italki.com
- Shovel snow through the winter
- Raise and sell dogs, cats, or rabbits. Chickens can also provide eggs for sell.
- Recycle cans and bottles
- Make homemade candles or soap and sell at a craft fair or through etsy.
- Make birdhouses to sell
- Make doll houses to sell
- Design and have t-shirts made to sell
- Computer repair or offer computer services
- Clean gutters
- Baby proof houses
- Leaf removal
- personal shopper
- personal organizer
- drop off and deliver dry cleaning
- create videos for business promotions

- sell specialty candy
- movie theater in your backyard
- paint fences
- power wash decks or houses
- Aerate Lawns
- Scan and digitalize photographs
- make digital scrapbooks for others
- grow houseplants and sell baby plants
- start vegetable plants from seeds and sell the plants for others
- Sell candy honor boxes- like a vending machine but depends on people to be honest when they take a candy.

Create a business Plan workbook page

Take a sheet of paper and answer these questions and formulate your business idea

1. What price will you charge for this service or idea?

2. What start up costs will you incur for this money making idea? Include supplies needed.

3. What will you do with the money you earn?

4. What is your long term financial goal? Short term financial goal?

5. Now take your ideas and create a plan that includes: Service provided, charges, responsibility and who will be in charge of money.

6. What idea do you have for money making:

7. How often can you work at this idea? Weekly, daily? How often are you available to do work with your current school, sports, hobbies schedule?

8. What service will you need to provide for making this idea work?

9. What skills do you think someone needs to accomplish this money making idea successfully?